LONDON TRANSPORT
in Colour 1965-1980

Kevin McCormack

Ian Allan
PUBLISHING

Front cover:

Spare wheels

To cover shortages Harrow Weald garage often had to borrow a green RLH
from the Country Area to assist on its lowbridge route 230, until the service
was replaced on 14 July 1969 by Merlin-operated flat-fare route H1. RLH17
was photographed in Headstone Drive, Wealdstone, on 7 June 1965.
Maurice Bateman

Back cover:

All aboard

Unnatural enthusiasm for a Swift is captured in High Street, Beckenham on
30 June 1977 as SMS673 is passed by RT4177. Route 54, operated by
Catford garage, would be converted to DMS operation on 22 April 1978,
while Swifts had replaced RFs on route 227 on 2 January 1971. *Chris Evans*

Previous page:

Hanging on

Although RTs were ousted from route 21A on 26 October 1968 as a result of
OMO, they survived on the 89 for almost another 10 years, conversion to
DMS (Fleetline) operation not being effected until 22 April 1978. With
some wishful thinking, RT1213 could be catching up with DMS2153 as it
climbs Well Hall Road, Eltham, on 19 May 1977. *Chris Evans*

Flying high

Photographed from the top deck of open-staircase ST922 working vintage
route 100, a Red Arrow of the terrestrial type, MBA597, proceeds along
Park Lane in April 1972 on route 500. This pioneer service began on 18 April
1966 and introduced Londoners to the concept of flat-fare, limited-stop
services carrying more standing than seated passengers. *Maurice Bateman*

First published 2007

ISBN (10) 0 7110 3203 3
ISBN (13) 978 0 7110 3203 3

© Ian Allan Publishing 2007

Published by Ian Allan Publishing

an imprint of Ian Allan Publishing Ltd, Hersham Surrey, KT12 4RG
Printed by Ian Allan Printing Ltd, Hersham Surrey, KT12 4RG

Code: 0706/B1

Visit the Ian Allan Publishing website at www.ianallanpublishing.com

Introduction

The period covered by this album was one of considerable change for London's buses. In 1965 doored double-deck buses were introduced experimentally in anticipation of widespread one-man operation (OMO). Then, on 1 January 1970, the Country Area bus services and Green Line coach network were transferred from London Transport (LT) to a newly formed National Bus Company (NBC) subsidiary, London Country Bus Services (LCBS). Between these dates London's tradition of a standardised and impeccably presented bus and coach fleet continued, as evidenced by the 1960s photographs in this book.

The 1970s, however, were notable for a general deterioration in the mechanical performance and external appearance of both the LT and LCBS fleets. The new generation of buses — off-the-shelf vehicles intended as replacements for the ageing RT and RF classes and additionally, in the case of LCBS, relatively new Routemasters — proved in many cases to be unreliable. Shortages of spare parts exacerbated the problem. By the mid-1970s LCBS was forced to hire buses from a variety of sources in order to maintain its scheduled services and even bought some ex-Southdown 'Queen Marys' for public use and ex-Ribble Titans for driver trainers. To a more limited extent LT had to do the same, although it was partly able to overcome its problems through extending the life of some RTs and RFs and buying up every surplus Routemaster that was available, repeating a process which had taken place in 1972 with the purchase of 34 second-hand RTs from LCBS. However, what proved to be a mechanic's nightmare became a delight to enthusiasts as RTs briefly returned to their old haunts and a variety of different coloured buses of unfamiliar origin appeared. Further interest was provided by the special liveries carried (mainly by Routemasters) for all-over advertising and certain commemorative events.

By the end of the 1970s, with the introduction by LT and LCBS of the next generation of buses, standards began to improve again, but these new vehicles have been largely excluded from this album, as they are more representative of a later period. Rather than illustrate every type of bus and coach operated by LT and LCBS between 1965 and 1980 I have sought instead to capture the flavour of the period: the transition from the old familiar fleet image to the largely unsuccessful new order which followed, prior to the brave new world of deregulation and privatisation which epitomised the 1980s and beyond and which transformed London's bus operations.

With the help of several photographers I have tried to present a colourful portrait of London buses in the period, covering as wide a geographical spread as available material allows, and with a few rarities thrown in for good measure. Those contributors who have augmented my photographs and who have kindly made available their precious and previously unpublished pictures for the enjoyment of readers of this book are: Maurice Bateman, Chris Evans (no, not *that* one!), Ray Webb, Ray Wilkinson, Mike Harries, Rodney Lissenden and Ian Pringle.

Kevin R. McCormack
Ashtead, Surrey
April 2007

Body shop
Viewed from the adjacent canal towpath in June 1965, five of the 43-strong RCL class of 30ft-long Green Line Routemaster coaches are lined up at Park Royal Vehicles Ltd following completion, prior to being moved to AEC at Southall for final inspection and testing. *Maurice Bateman*

3

Borrowed time

Two photographs which emphasise the reliance on loaned vehicles in Surrey in the latter years of the 1970s. In the first, taken on 17 April 1977, LCBS's Chelsham garage plays host to RMC1473 and BN37 standing between two Maidstone Borough Council Massey-bodied Leyland Atlanteans, with LR19, one of 20 ex-Ribble Burlingham-bodied Leyland PD3/4s purchased for driver training, on the end. The second features West Croydon bus station on 8 January 1976, with RM1565 sandwiched between a Bournemouth Corporation Weymann-bodied Daimler Fleetline and a Southend Transport East Lancs-bodied PD3, the latter on hire to LT.
Chris Evans

Works outing

Left: Two staff buses, RT329 and RT1866, at Tring garage stand ready to ferry LT workers to Aldenham in May 1966. The overhanging canopy identifies the former as an RT3-bodied bus. The withdrawal of the last two RT3s from passenger service on 1 May 1965 left just four, including RT329, in LT stock, all being used as staff buses. *Maurice Bateman*

Luckless Leylands

Above: After withdrawal of the early-bodied AEC RTs, the axe fell next on the RTW class, followed closely by the RTL class, the last of which were withdrawn from public service on 30 November 1968. RTL407 is seen on 13 April 1968 in Cambridge Avenue, at the Kilburn Park Station terminus of route 142. *Maurice Bateman*

Hidden horrors
LT's traditional Lincoln-green livery, with new yellow relief (enhanced by the aluminium trim which the related class of Swifts lacked) almost gave the Merlins an air of respectability! In this June 1969 shot MB101 waits at the Leavesden Road, Watford, terminus of route 335 before setting off for Windsor. *Maurice Bateman*

Bringing up the rear

FRM1 follows XA7 to Tottenham as both buses cross back over the River Thames using Blackfriars Bridge after travelling over Westminster Bridge on their journey from Victoria. FRM1, the unique rear-engined Routemaster, entered service on 26 June 1967 and is seen here three days later. XA7, one of 50 Park Royal-bodied Leyland Atlanteans, was taking part in comparative trials with new RMLs, route 76 being the second service chosen for the exchanges. *Maurice Bateman*

Hard drive

Above: Kingston's RFs, which provided drivers with the benefit of preselector gearboxes, were replaced on route 206 from 22 August 1976 by new Fulwell-based BL-class Bristol LHs with manual gearboxes. However, the Bristols lasted only a short time on this service, which was withdrawn on 28 October 1978 and replaced by a revised route 215. This photograph, taken on 10 July 1978, depicts BL39 at Esher Common, opposite the War Memorial in Lammas Lane. *Chris Evans*

Out of the Country

Right: Although it would be another 17 months before the last LCBS Routemaster was withdrawn from normal public service the diminishing fleet was already unloved by LCBS (but not by LT, which couldn't wait to get its hands on them!) when this shot was taken at Garston garage on 25 October 1978. In the foreground is RML2451, a driver trainer, and the other RMs, surrounded by new Atlanteans and Nationals, are RMLs 2432 and 2423 and ex-Green Line coach RMC1502. *Chris Evans*

Home from home

Above: The combination of a low railway bridge in nearby Chertsey Road and the need on three Country Area routes (436, 436A and 461) for a higher capacity than RFs were able to provide brought provincial-standard lowbridge AEC Regents to Staines. Allocated to Addlestone garage and with bodywork built at Weymann's Addlestone factory, RLH32 (since preserved) stands outside the former Staines West railway station on 22 April 1965. LCBS would withdraw its last RLHs from public service on 31 July 1970. *Maurice Bateman*

Must be a puncture!

Right: Since everyone knows that it was only Fleetlines, Merlins and Swifts that suffered mechanical failure in the 1970s, this image of an RT disgracing itself is particularly astonishing! An AEC Matador master breakdown tender with 5-ton crane — 750P of 1949 vintage — comes to the aid of RT921 at Shepherd's Bush Green in August 1971. *Maurice Bateman*

Tilling time

Left: ST922 takes a break in Horse Guards Avenue, off Victoria Embankment, in April 1972, while operating vintage route 100. Having entered service with Thomas Tilling in 1930, this bus was absorbed by LT in 1933 and withdrawn from passenger service in 1946, continuing as a mobile canteen until 1954. Rescued from a scrapyard in 1966 and subsequently restored, this historic vehicle went on to provide many years of reliable operation on this special service and now lives in retirement at Cobham Bus Museum. *Author's collection*

No grand finale

Above: Given that AEC had produced successful bus types for LT since 1912, it was a pity that the manufacturer's last effort was the unfortunate, underpowered Swift. SMS353, dating from 1971, negotiates Marble Arch in November 1980, providing cover during engineering works on the Central Line tube. Although the Swift was shorter than its close relative, the Merlin, it appeared longer through having more side windows. *Author's collection*

Odds-on favourite

Left: Pride of place on the Derby Day special service on 1 June 1977 went to RT3461, loaned by Chelsham garage and seen here at Epsom Downs. It was a great surprise when LCBS recertified four RTs in the summer of 1977, repainting three of them, including this vehicle, in NBC corporate livery. Unfortunately its public-service rejuvenation was short-lived, due to an easing in LCBS's vehicle shortage, and the bus was transferred to the training fleet in September 1977. *Chris Evans*

Top secret

Above: In a clever move which enabled the same sightseeing vehicles to be used throughout the year despite the vagaries of the British climate, LT introduced the DMO class, complete with detachable roofs. Maintaining its 1970s *penchant* for obtaining second-hand vehicles, LT bought seven of these 1965-built Daimler Fleetlines from Bournemouth Transport in 1977 and used them on its Round London Sightseeing Tour until 1981.
On 25 July 1980 DMO1 was photographed in Buckingham Palace Road, alongside Victoria Station, heading back empty to Stockwell garage. DMO3 is preserved by Ensignbus of Purfleet. *Chris Evans*

Ware to get off
… in this case Fanshawe Crescent, terminus of local Hertford route 395.
RT4781, seen here in early LCBS days (1971), was one of 144 surplus new
buses built in 1954 and was kept in store at Loughton garage, not entering
service until June 1959. *Ray Wilkinson*

Viewfinder
The Round London Sightseeing Tour also used seven hired D9s built by the Birmingham & Midland Motor Omnibus Co, the operating arm of which was better known as Midland Red. Looking every bit like an authentic LT bus, complete with RF bullseye on the radiator grille, OM1, dating from 1960, proceeds along Pall Mall in May 1980, with the National Gallery in Trafalgar Square in the background. *Author*

Wheels of fortune

Above: After serving as a store shed for 39 years this Dodson-bodied Dennis of 1925 vintage, D142, was very lucky to be rescued, united with a suitable chassis and put back into service. The bus, originally belonging to the Dominion Omnibus Co (taken over in 1926 by the London General Omnibus Co) was withdrawn as early as 1931. Seen here opposite Charing Cross station in the Strand while working vintage route 100 in August 1980, this vehicle now resides at Cobham Bus Museum. *Author*

Country cousin

Right: Believe it or not, these vehicles are related, both being Park Royal-bodied AECs. Routemaster RM2083 is joined by Green Line Reliance RP88 in Langham Place (at the top of Regent Street) in May 1973. LCBS ordered 90 of these coaches, primarily as OMO replacements for Routemaster coaches, but their reign on Green Line routes was relatively short: most were relegated to bus work when new luxury coaches were introduced from 1977, and the last RP ran in passenger service in February 1984. *Author*

Thirty-year stint

Route 94 was the longest continuously worked RT route (1948-78) and also the third-last to be served by the type. Full RM conversion was effected on 27 August 1978, the day after this photograph was taken in Southborough Lane, Petts Wood. However, RT2143 lived on to become a 'skid bus' at Chiswick Works. It was finally withdrawn in March 1985, leaving just two other RTs in stock for a little longer. *Author*

Regents Parked

RLHs 62, 59, 74, 60 and 63 stand idle at Harrow Weald garage in early 1966 during the ban on overtime and rest-day working prompted by savage cuts in Central Area services due to declining passenger numbers. Along with many other services across London the RLH-operated 230 was suspended from 30 January to 20 March 1966, although for most of this time it was covered by an independent operator, Valliant Direct Coaches. Following withdrawal these five RLHs were all exported to the USA, where RLHs 60 and 62 are believed to be still extant. *Maurice Bateman*

In the line of duty
In this view of the interior of Palmers Green garage in October 1977 the
photographer, flanked by a Routemaster and a B20 'quiet' Fleetline, has
captured a row of RTs, including 4624 and 3342, ready to work route 102
(Golders Green–Chingford). This service was fully converted to RM
operation on 4 March 1978. *Ray Webb*

Just the ticket
In this second shot inside Palmers Green garage in October 1977 RM615
is the subject of a much-needed waste-paper-removal exercise. Route 298A,
a new service from Turnpike Lane to Oakwood introduced on 7 September
1968, was converted from RT to RM operation on 24 January 1970.
Ray Webb

Another fine mess

MD34, seen here in Praed Street, Paddington, on 22 May 1976, proudly proclaims itself to be 'Another new bus for London'. However, the MD class of 164 Scania/MCW Metropolitans proved to be another 1970s disaster due to problems with corrosion and spare-parts shortages.

The first 12 entered service on 22 March 1976, nine went to the breakers in August 1980, and the last one ran on 25 June 1983! Ironically these Anglo-Swedish vehicles had been ordered partly because of the poor performance of the DMS class. *Chris Evans*

Last posting

Barking garage was the final home of the RT family in public service, hosting the last two routes (87 and 62). Route 87 was converted to RM operation on 28 October 1978, apart from one Saturday duty. Standing alongside RT2773 in this view is RT3911, which has just joined the Barking fleet from Harrow Weald following the conversion of route 140 on 15 July 1978. *Ray Webb*

Outstanding achiever

Above: Looking immaculate, RF315 is seen here at Harrow-on-the-Hill on 8 August 1966, the first day of new OMO route 136. This brought a bus service to the top of the hill for the first time since 1914; it was also the first single-deck Central Area route since October 1934 to be numbered outside the 200 series. Fifty years after its entry into service in 1952, RF315 was still working a bus route, albeit not an LT one, and although now residing in Ensign's Museum, its operational career may not yet be over. *Maurice Bateman*

In the red

Right: A temporary shortage of green RTs caused the Country Bus & Coach Department to borrow from the Central Area to cover Stevenage's expanding local services pending the arrival of green RTs displaced by new RMLs at High Wycombe and Garston in 1966. RT2912 was photographed in March 1966 at Stevenage bus station. *Maurice Bateman*

29

Off-colour

Left: An experiment to speed up the repainting process by eliminating the light-grey central relief band was tried out in 1968 on Routemasters. Luckily this dull, all-over red livery was not adopted for the RM and RT fleets, but it was nevertheless considered suitable for the DMS class of Daimler Fleetlines, introduced from 2 January 1971. This view at Gillingham Street garage, Victoria, depicts RM496, one of six Highgate Routemasters outshopped from Aldenham Works in all-over red and restored to normal livery three months later. *Maurice Bateman*

Relief workers

Above: Four RMLs line up for duty at Windsor garage on 27 March 1967, three of them ready for Green Line relief duty on routes originating from Windsor. This was in the days when these coach services crossed London, route 704 going to Tunbridge Wells and route 718 to Harlow, both via Victoria. Note that RML2318 (right) has been given the wrong style of radiator badge. *Maurice Bateman*

Seaside specials

Above and right: During the period covered by this book red Routemasters were a familiar sight in unfamiliar places, undertaking day trips on summer weekends. In this view from June 1980 RT885 was about to be photographed alongside Leyland National SNB502 at Dorking (Deepdene) when a Willesden Routemaster heading for the South Coast unexpectedly entered the viewfinder. The SNB was deputising for RF202 on the Sunday ramblers' service and must have caused havoc in the narrow lanes of the Surrey Hills. The second view was taken in Brighton in May 1980 and shows two RMs about to be passed by Southdown 0813, a Brush-bodied Leyland TD1 dating from 1929. *Author (both)*

Spot the difference

Left and above: The date, route, location and vehicle type are all the same and the buses are consecutively numbered. Both RF602 and RF603, seen here at Golders Green station, were transferred from the Country Area to Muswell Hill, along with 10 others, on 1 January 1969, still in green livery.

RF603 (nowadays preserved by Ensignbus) was painted red at Aldenham in June 1969 (although there is something odd about its bullseye radiator-cap cover plate), RF602 following suit in July. *Maurice Bateman (both)*

The name game

Above: At the end of 1969, to meet the expanding needs of Stevenage New Town and also to minimise expensive road-building, a subsidised local bus network was introduced. Marketed first as 'Blue Arrow', using three Daimler Fleetlines (XF6-8), and then as the 'No fuss bus', the services were expanded and rebranded as 'Superbus' on 31 July 1971. This operation started with five Swifts (SM495-9) and two Metro-Scanias (MS1 and MS2), and this shot depicts MS1 leaving Stevenage bus station. On 26 April 1980 the town services were re-branded yet again, this time as 'StevenageBus'. *John May*

Training coach

Right: As well as purchasing the entire British Airways Routemaster fleet LT acquired almost the entire LCBS Routemaster fleet and wasted no time in employing the standard-length former Green Line coaches (RMCs) on non-passenger duties (initially without repainting them) in order to release back into service RTs with a current Certificate of Fitness (CoF). On 30 March 1978 Catford trainer RMC1494 leads RML2314 (at the time still owned by LCBS) into High Street, Croydon. *Chris Evans*

Palace visitors
Left: Plumstead's RT1654 shares the night life with a Routemaster on route 137 and a DMS on route 108A at Crystal Palace. RTs were replaced by RMs on route 122 on 22 April 1978, a bad day for RTs which also saw their replacement on routes 54, 89 and 146. *Ray Webb*

For whom the bell tolls
Right: Contrasting with the majority of surviving LCBS RTs, which were generally battered and scruffy by this time, Windsor's highly presentable RT1009 sets off from Old Windsor (The Bells of Ouseley) on a short working of route 441 to Hedgerley Village in September 1976. Sadly this vehicle's five-year CoF was to expire in March 1977, prompting its withdrawal from service. *Author*

Fat boy and slim

Left: Two very different members of the RT family bask in the morning sunshine at Harrow Weald garage in June 1966. Roofbox RT4223 is one of the 300 Saunders-bodied vehicles, the last of which ran in public service in March 1971, while RTW441, operating as a driver trainer, displays its extra 6in width as it stands alongside. *Maurice Bateman*

Crew cut

Above: RF529, seen at Abridge on 1 April 1965, belonged to the batch numbered RF502-38, which were converted to OMO, with the addition of doors, in 1959 and promptly stored due to trade-union opposition; although the Country Area had an existing OMO agreement the Central Area one had lapsed following the withdrawal of the red Leyland Cubs in 1949. The RFs later re-entered service as crew buses until OMO was eventually implemented for Central Area single-deckers in November 1964, North Street, Romford's route 250 being among the first four to be converted. *Maurice Bateman*

George the first

One of the most attractive liveries ever worn by London buses was surely the 150th-anniversary livery based on the colours applied to George Shillibeer's pioneer 'Omnibus', which began operating between Marylebone and the Bank of England in 1829. Twelve service RMs and one DM wore this livery. On 18 March 1979, 15 days after the privately sponsored 'Shillibeers' appeared on the streets, RM2186 is seen in St Johns Road, Clapham Junction. *Author's collection*

Putting on the style

By the mid-1960s LT considered that Green Line coach services needed a more modern image. One of the problems was that, although new Routemaster coaches had taken over some of the services from 1962, RFs were still the mainstay and, having been introduced in October 1951, were beginning to look dated. Consequently, starting with RF136 in March 1966, 175 of them were modernised, including RF82, seen outside the former East Surrey Traction Co offices on the corner of Lesbourne Road and Bell Street, Reigate, in August 1969. *Mike Harries*

In your face

Above: This is an example of unexpected oncoming traffic in St Alban's Road, Watford, photographed from a car window! GS42 has several claims to fame which include being the last of the 84 diminutive Guy Specials to be overhauled at Aldenham (emerging on 10 January 1966), working the final LT/LCBS GS journey (on 30 March 1972) and winning 1st prize at Ashtead Village Day in June 2005, when it competed against several historic vehicles including the author's Austin Seven! This view from June 1970 shows the bus shortly after it was transferred (again) to Garston as a trainer, prior to re-entering public service in March 1971 in place of GS17, sharing route 336A (Rickmansworth–Loudwater Estate) with GS33. *Ray Wilkinson*

Fire and hire

Right: Passing through Chiswick Works' historic iron gates in July 1978 is privately owned RT191, one of 14 preserved RT-family vehicles borrowed by LT at various times between 4 April and 1 November 1978 for driver training. This was to release from training duties those LT-owned RTs which still had CoFs so that they could re-enter public service to replace operational RTs with expiring CoFs. *Author*

Back number

Left: In September/October 1965 routes 73 and 321 were chosen to test public reaction to the elimination of all route information (save the number) at the rear of non-OMO buses, as seen here on RT4550 in Exchange Road, Watford. The intention was apparently to restrict the quantity of blinds requiring alteration when the 'via' points changed (for OMO vehicles it was to save the driver from having to vacate his driving position). The idea was adopted, but with an outsize route number in the full 'via' box and the destination blind retained. *Maurice Bateman*

Fair dodger

Above: Pinner's annual street fair causes major disruption to bus services. Before West End Lane was capable of handling buses route 209 had to be diverted away from Pinner and Pinner Green, whilst the 183s were truncated either side of the Fair. Seen in Elm Park Road on the occasion of the 1966 event, RT311 is making a three-point turn by Pinner police station to return to Northwood. The showman's bus is CRJ 541, an ex-Salford Leyland Titan. *Maurice Bateman*

Diverted Daimlers

Left: Delivered in 1972 and becoming LCBS's first new double-deckers, the AF class of 11 Daimler Fleetlines were ordered by Western Welsh and spent their entire operational lives of up to 10 years at Godstone garage working chiefly on route 410. On 4 May 1978 AF8 was photographed at Old Coulsdon pond, having strayed onto route 409. *Chris Evans*

Reigning supreme

Above: The Routemasters say it all — this is Catford bus garage! Route 47 became exclusively RM-operated when the RTs which had been helping out were withdrawn from Bromley and Catford garages on 27 August 1978. *Ray Webb*

Shining example

Although the former trolleybus depot at Stonebridge Park stopped using RTs in public service from 14 May 1971 it continued to receive them as visitors for a few more years, in particular LT and LCBS trainers (must have been a good canteen there!), as well as housing withdrawn buses and some lucky examples for recertification. In contrast with Stonebridge Park's resident turnover vehicle (the largely windowless RT lurking in the background, which replaced 1036TV, ex RT106) RT693 looks magnificent after a full repaint in 1975, putting adjacent SMS437 and RM244 in the shade. *Author*

Grand Nationals

LT purchased six Leyland Nationals for trials in 1973 and may well have left it at that, had it not been for the unreliability of the Swifts and the urgent need for some replacement single-deckers. The Nationals proved themselves to be competent performers, so from 1976 LT bought a further 500, mainly to replace Swifts but also some DMSs. This shot, taken on 24 July 1979 at South Harrow station, shows the old order in the form of SMS331 and SMS replacements LS308 and LS321. *Maurice Bateman*

Blaze of glory

Left: Forty years (bar four months) of public-service RT working in London came to an end on 7 April 1979, when Barking garage's route 62 was converted (during the day) to RM operation following a minor re-routing to accommodate the latter type's extra 6in width. RT1301, seen earlier in the year looking as though it has been the subject of an arson attack, was one of six RTs which operated the route on the final morning, prior to a ceremonial cavalcade taking place in the afternoon. *Ray Webb*

Finishing post

Above: All-over advertising on London buses was a phenomenon which started in 1969 and lasted into the 1980s but is mainly associated with the period 1971-4, which saw 25 LT RMs and RMLs and three LCBS RMCs bedecked in liveries varying from the sublime to the ridiculous. Here RML2560, standing beside a Victorian octagonal pillar box, has brought Ladbrokes to Ladbroke Grove, where route 15 terminated beside The Eagle public house. *Ian Pringle*

Box number

Above: The superb condition of these Leyland RTLs at the Woodford Bridge terminus of route 10 from Victoria in May 1965 belies the fact that they had only a limited period of LT service remaining. For this reason RTL246 had been fitted at overhaul with an old RT10 roofbox body, releasing a newer body to be fitted to a longer-serving RT. Meanwhile, its neighbour, RTL301, is seen with a non-roofbox body as carried originally by all 1,631 members of the class apart from the prototype, RTL501. *Maurice Bateman*

Information underload

Right: Perhaps instead of bothering to test public reaction to the loss of route information on the rear of buses (see page 46) LT could simply have sought the opinion of RLH passengers who were provided with no information at the back except, if they were lucky, an almost invisible route number stencil. RLH63, which would later be exported to the USA and whose ultimate fate is unknown, stands at the Rayners Lane terminus in June 1966. *Maurice Bateman*

Same but different

Above and right: Apart from livery, there was little to distinguish the 50-strong XA class of Leyland Atlanteans from the eight XF Daimler Fleetlines, as, despite mechanical differences, both types were fitted with similar Park Royal bodywork. Comparative tests were set up between the XAs and XFs (also involving RMLs) in which the latter showed their

superiority. In 1973 all 50 XAs were exported to Hong Kong, where they operated until replaced by redundant DMS Fleetlines in 1979/80. These views show XA3 and XA22 at the Grosvenor Road, Pimlico, terminus of route 24, while, in less urban surroundings, XF7 climbs away from Bell Street, Reigate. *Robin Hannay collection / Mike Harries*

Unkempt in Kent

Above: A study of visual dilapidation is provided by Northfleet garage's RML2343 at Gravesend Pier on 24 September 1979, prior to new ANs' taking over the 480 service in November 1979. LCBS withdrew its last Routemasters from normal service in February 1980, and RML2446 and RMC1512 operated a commemorative farewell tour on 1 March 1980. *Chris Evans*

White knight

Right: At Sevenoaks station a Royal Blue Bristol MW coach, complete with antimacassars on the seats and skylights in the roof, provides bus passengers on route 483 with a taste of luxury on 7 May 1976. Because of chronic bus shortages LCBS had hired several such coaches in 1975 and concentrated them on Dunton Green garage, which had drivers trained on manual gearboxes and spare conductors, the latter being necessary because the doors were manually operated. *Chris Evans*

Contrast in coaches

Left and above: LCBS's last two public-service RFs (202 and 221) saw frequent use on Green Line coach services towards the end of their long careers. Immaculate RF221, an unmodernised coach in its 25th year (and which was to remain in service until October 1978), passes Reeves Corner, Croydon, on 4 July 1977. Meanwhile, a few months earlier, on 5 February 1977 in Park Lane, brand-new RS4, a Plaxton-bodied AEC Reliance, represents the improved Green Line image which was to involve the replacement of the existing fleet (consisting mainly of Leyland Nationals) by luxury coaches, starting in January 1977. *Chris Evans*

Little and large

Above: In February 1966 RM1008, still in largely original condition, shares Edgware station forecourt with RF455. Another of its type to enjoy a long active life, the RF had entered service at Sidcup garage in January 1953 and would be withdrawn at Hounslow in April 1977. *Maurice Bateman*

No protection

Right: Due mainly to size limitations in the days when covered accommodation for service buses was the norm, Seven Kings garage retained a 100%-RT allocation as late as February 1976. However, while the garage was being rebuilt in 1974 some buses were parked in Goodmayes station yard, with tragic consequences for RTs 526 and 4035, which were destroyed by arsonists. This view from February 1974 features six RTs neatly lined up in their somewhat bleak temporary surroundings, RTs 4728 and 2556 being the two nearest the camera. *Maurice Bateman*

Born too late

Above: Nowadays an active exhibit in London's Transport Museum, FRM1 was the prototype for a new generation of front-entrance, rear-engined Routemasters built to LT's own specification, until politics dictated that off-the-peg buses should be purchased instead. The vehicle was converted to OMO for use from 19 December 1969 on Croydon garage's route 233, which a month earlier had become London's first double-deck OMO service. The bus is pictured leaving West Croydon bus station in February 1971, a few weeks before this single-vehicle route was converted to SMS operation, the need for a more frequent service necessitating an additional vehicle. With its combined single entrance/exit FRM1 was incompatible with other modern doored buses save those of the XA and XF classes. *Mike Harries*

Little change

Right: LCBS operations at Dorking in September 1975 still had an LT flavour about them. Besides the LT bus-stop flag (largely concealed by the signboard), the Leyland Atlantean, AN37, has an LT-style front destination display, and route 425 is being worked by a hired LT Merlin, MBS70. The initial order for 90 ANs mirrored the order for 90 RPs, all having Park Royal bodywork utilising some common parts, notably the windscreen and lower front panels. *Mike Harries*

Standing proud

Above: The crew of RT4537 pose beside their steed in York Road, Ilford, on 14 April 1967. Route 144, with RTs supplied by Walthamstow and Wood Green garages, was converted to DMS operation on 5 January 1974, yet by the end of that year nearly a thousand RTs remained licensed for service, and it was becoming clear that they would soldier on for at least a few more years. Indeed the last RT withdrawals coincided with the first DMS withdrawals, such that examples of both classes could be seen standing alongside one another in the scrapyard. *Maurice Bateman*

Fit for a queen

Right: Privileged to be carrying HM The Queen Mother, if only in pictorial form (!), Brixton's RTW336 passes through Selsdon on its journey from Victoria to Croydon garage on 13 March 1966. RMs took over on 15 May 1966, when the last four RTW routes, all operated by Brixton garage, succumbed. Nearly 40 years later Brixton bade farewell to its RMs, having been the last garage to operate the type in normal service. *Rodney Lissenden*

Mixed midriffs

Scheduled RF operation on Green Line coach services ended in October 1975, Leyland Nationals taking over. However, right through to July 1979, when the last operational example (RF202, which even bore Green Line fleetnames) suffered a gearbox failure, RFs still worked as substitutes on these services. In their later years the surviving modernised RFs could be found with pale green, bright yellow or white central relief bands. In this view, recorded at Leatherhead garage on 2 July 1977, two varieties are displayed by, from left to right, RFs 79, 218 and 54.
Chris Evans

Pay and display

To mark HM The Queen's Silver Jubilee in 1977, 25 of the newest standard-length Routemasters then going through overhaul were painted silver. As with the Shillibeer buses two years later, the costs of this exercise were defrayed by sponsorship from a variety of companies whose products were advertised on the vehicles in question. Temporarily renumbered SRM24, Stockwell garage's RM1922, closely followed by RM2024, turns into Park Lane from Oxford Street at Marble Arch on 14 April 1977. *Chris Evans*

Shining example

Above: LT's limited recertification programme for RTs in the early/mid-1970s ran for four years and enabled vehicles such as RT1808, seen leaving Walthamstow Central station in summer 1975, to recover some of their former glory. OMO came to route 34 on 10 September 1977, when DMSs replaced RTs, marking the end of RT operation at Walthamstow garage. *Author's collection*

Class distinction

Right: Although vehicles classified DMS were OMO, there were three other variants within the class: crew-operated DMs, dual-purpose DMs reclassified D and dual-purpose DMSs reclassified DS. This photograph, taken outside Southall (HW) bus garage in Uxbridge Road, shows DM1216, complete with conductor, working alongside RM2191 on route 207 in September 1980. *Author's collection*

Lost liveries

NBC killed off the traditional colour schemes of its subsidiary companies in the interests of maintaining a corporate image, as evidenced here in June 1978 at Crawley bus station, where LCBS and Southdown vehicles are virtually indistinguishable. Demonstrating why Green Line desperately needed a new image, scruffy RP71 is working the prestigious inter-airport 727 service, which had been officially converted to RS operation the previous September. Behind is Leyland Atlantean AN146 on route 429, which would be renumbered C7 on 1 July 1978, when Crawley's town services were re-branded as 'C-Line'. *Author's collection*

Reduced status

Following its purchase of virtually the entire LCBS Routemaster fleet, LT made the surprising decision to convert 40 of the RCL class of ex Green Line coaches to work as buses on route 149, replacing DMs. The conversion work included removal of the luggage racks, twin headlights and platform doors — quite an expense for what turned out to be only four years' service. Seen in Lambeth Palace Road, with the Houses of Parliament as a backdrop, RCL2251 prepares to cross Lambeth Bridge in August 1980, the first month of RCL operation on this service. *Harry Luff*

Sea change

Above: Eastbourne Borough Council AEC Regent V No 60 was one of three such buses which came inland for a spell of duty to help alleviate LCBS's chronic shortage of operational vehicles. Further down this queue of traffic near Orpington station on 7 May 1976 is Swift SM530. *Chris Evans*

Keeping down appearances

Right: During the peak period of LT's lack of serviceable buses (1974-7) 17 bus garages that had dispensed with RTs welcomed them back again, however tired they looked. Holloway's RT2052 has a full load as it approaches Hyde Park Corner from Piccadilly on 14 April 1977.
On the right is SNC192, one of 87 Leyland National 'suburban coaches' specifically purchased for Green Line service in the years 1974-6, only to be superseded by AEC Reliance (RB/RS) coaches from January 1977. *Chris Evans*

Lack of grey matter

Above: From May 1965 the cream central relief band on Central Area red buses was replaced by pastel grey, but this was considered too pale, and from November 1965 a darker 'mist grey' was used. Pictured in Eastcote Lane, between South Ruislip and South Harrow, resplendent RT3806 shows off the earlier grey (looking more like white) during the summer of 1965. The person standing by the nearside front wing could be the conductress about to insert her card into the red time-clock, a procedure intended to deter early running. *Maurice Bateman*

Conversation piece

Right: The driver is no doubt extolling the virtues of his new Green Line coach to admiring colleagues outside Romford garage as he prepares to set off behind the wheel of RCL2218, the first member of the class, on 3 June 1965. Unfortunately these superb machines were introduced too late to be fully appreciated, because the subsequent reduction in the popularity of Green Line services brought about by increasing car ownership dictated an urgent need for OMO vehicles to maintain economic viability. *Maurice Bateman*

Home truth

A couple of months before the author's local route was restructured and renumbered (on 28 October 1978), SM457, representing AEC's last and probably least successful vehicle type, travels along Barnett Wood Lane, Ashtead. The vehicle has just passed the author's family (prior to expansion), visible behind the shopper. Leatherhead garage had the dubious pleasure of receiving the first Swifts delivered to LCBS, introducing them on the 418 service from 27 June 1970 in place of RTs. *Author*

Cutting a dash

It is 4.45pm on 5 December 1977 at West Croydon bus station, and Chelsham's immaculate RT604, LCBS's oldest bus, is in charge of a peak-hour Express working of the 403 service, which route had been officially converted to RCL operation in July 1977. Hopes that this bus would outlast its LT contemporaries in passenger service were dashed in September 1978 when it suffered engine failure and no repairs or replacement engine were forthcoming. Fortunately the vehicle has been privately preserved.
Chris Evans

Still standing

Hardly any ex-LT Country Area bus garages remain today, so it is all the more remarkable that among the few survivors is Swanley garage, which pre-dates LT, having been built for the East Surrey Traction Co (despite being in Kent!). This view dates from July 1969. Since the demise of LCBS the building has seen further use for garaging buses but is currently unoccupied. *Dave Brown*